# Children's Songs & CARTOON Classics

### Arranged by Richard Bradley

**Richard Bradley** is one of the world's best-known and best-selling arrangers of piano music for print. His success can be attributed to years of experience as a teacher and his understanding of students' and players' needs. His innovative piano methods for adults (*Bradley's How to Play Piano* – Adult Books 1, 2, and 3) and kids (*Bradley for Kids* – Red, Blue, and Green Series) not only teach the instrument, but they also teach musicianship each step of the way.

Originally from the Chicago area, Richard completed his undergraduate and graduate work at the Chicago Conservatory of Music and Roosevelt University. After college, Richard became a print arranger for Hansen Publications and later became music director of Columbia Pictures Publications. In 1977, he co-founded his own publishing company, Bradley Publications, which is now exclusively distributed worldwide by Warner Bros. Publications.

Richard is equally well known for his piano workshops, clinics, and teacher training seminars. He was a panelist for the first and second Keyboard Teachers' National Video Conferences, which were attended by more than 20,000 piano teachers throughout the United States.

The home video version of his adult teaching method, *How to Play Piano With Richard Bradley*, was nominated for an American Video Award as Best Music Instruction Video, and, with sales climbing each year since its release, it has brought thousands of adults to—or back to—piano lessons. Still, Richard advises, "The video can only get an adult started and show them what they can do. As they advance, all students need direct input from an accomplished teacher."

Additional Richard Bradley videos aimed at other than the beginning pianist include *How to Play Blues Piano* and *How to Play Jazz Piano*. As a frequent television talk show guest on the subject of music education, Richard's many appearances include "Hour Magazine" with Gary Collins, "The Today Show," and "Mother's Day" with former "Good Morning America" host Joan Lunden, as well as dozens of local shows.

Project Manager: *Zobeída Pérez*

Art Design: *Carmen Fortunato*

LOONEY TUNES, characters, names and all related indicia are trademarks of Warner Bros. © 2001

© 2001 BRADLEY PUBLICATIONS
All Rights Assigned to and Controlled by WARNER BROS. PUBLICATIONS U.S. INC.,
15800 NW 48th Avenue, Miami, FL 33014
All Rights Reserved

Bradley Publications
a division of
R&R Communications, Inc.

# Contents

# I Taut I Taw a Puddy-Tat
## (I Thought I Saw a Pussy-Cat)

Words and Music by
ALAN LIVINGSTON, BILL MAY
and WARREN FOSTER
*Arranged by Richard Bradley*

Moderately ♩ = 132

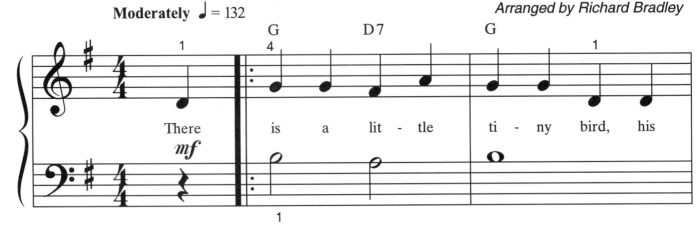

There is a lit-tle ti-ny bird, his

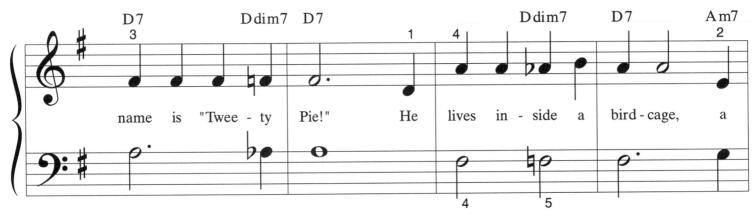

name is "Twee-ty Pie!" He lives in-side a bird-cage, a

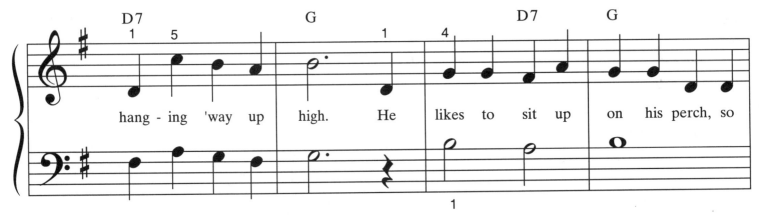

hang-ing 'way up high. He likes to sit up on his perch, so

hap-py and so gay. But, when a cat comes af-ter him, you'll

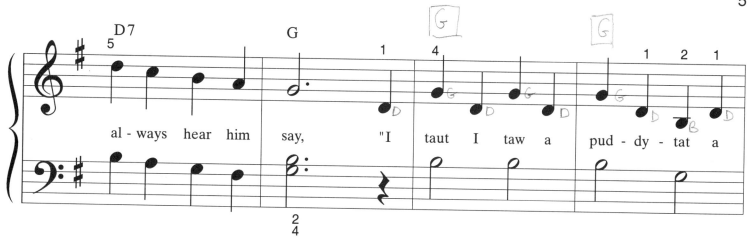

al - ways hear him say, "I taut I taw a pud - dy - tat a

creep - in' up on me._____ I did, I taw a pud - dy - tat as

plain as he could be. There be.

**Verse 2:**
There is a great big bad old cat,
Sylvester is his name,
He only has one aim in life,
And that is very plain.
He dreams of catching Tweety Pie
And eating him one day,
But just as he gets close enough,
Tweety gets away.
*(To Chorus:)*

**Verse 3:**
Tweety sometimes takes a walk
And goes outside his cage,
But he gets back before the cat,
And throws him in a rage.
Sylvester'd love to eat that bird
If he could just get near,
But ev'rytime that he comes by,
This is all he'll hear,
*(To Chorus:)*

**Verse 4:**
And when he sings that little song,
His mistress knows he's home,
She grabs her broom and brings it down
Upon Sylvester's dome.
So there's no need of worrying,
He lives just like a king,
And puddy-tats can't hurt that bird
As long as he can sing,
*(To Chorus:)*

# Woody Woodpecker

From the Cartoon Television Series

Words and Music by
GEORGE TIBBLES and RAMEY IDRISS
*Arranged by Richard Bradley*

# Mairzy Doats

Words and Music by
**MILTON DRAKE, AL HOFFMAN** and **JERRY LIVINGSTON**
*Arranged by Richard Bradley*

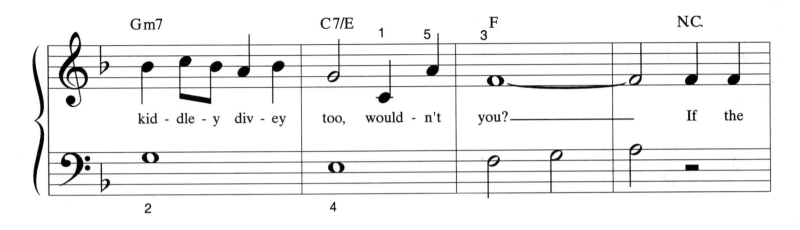

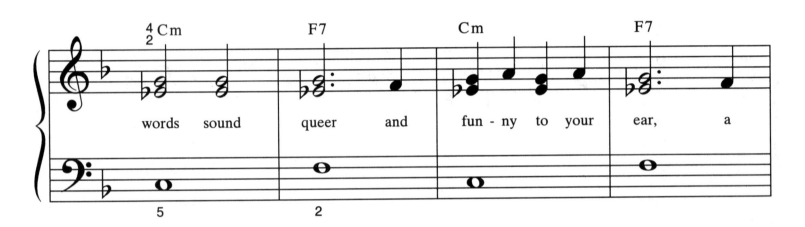

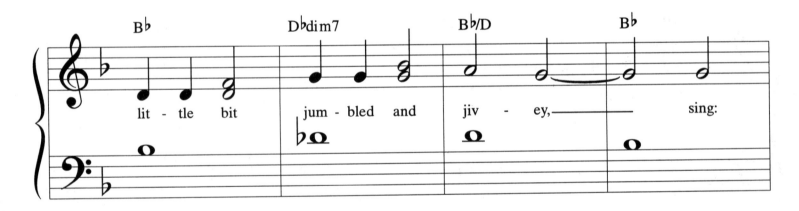

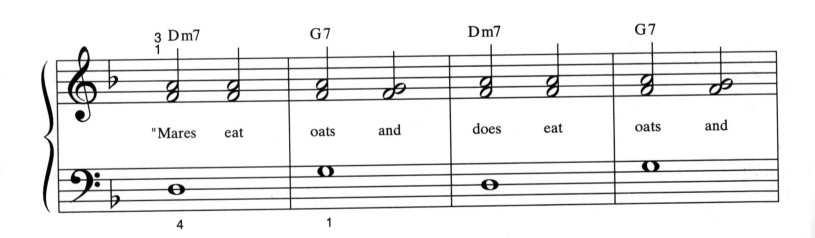

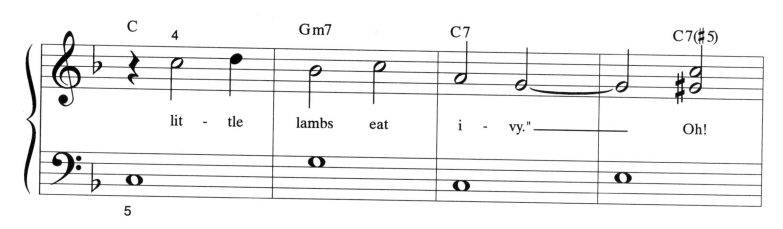

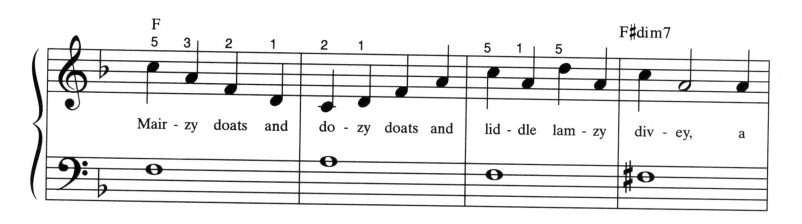

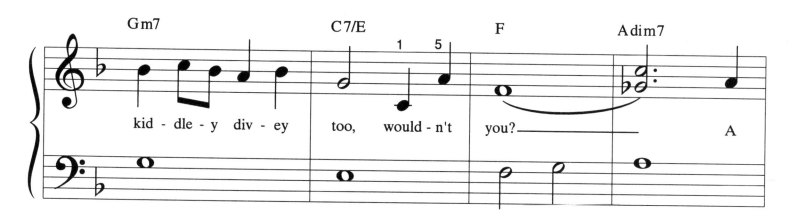

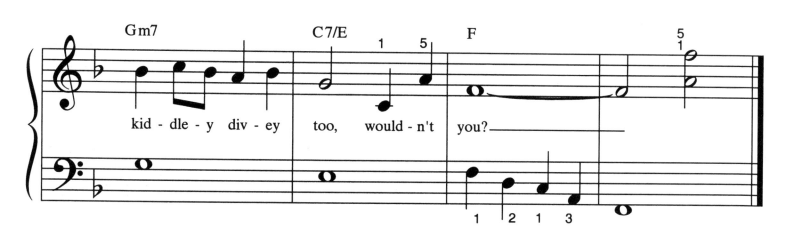

# Over the Rainbow

Featured in the MGM Picture *The Wizard Of Oz*

Lyric by E.Y. HARBURG
Music by HAROLD ARLEN
*Arranged by Richard Bradley*

# We're Off to See the Wizard
## (The Wonderful Wizard of Oz)

Featured in the MGM Picture *The Wizard of Oz*

Lyric by E.Y. HARBURG
Music by HAROLD ARLEN
*Arranged by Richard Bradley*

# The ABC Song

TRADITIONAL
*Arranged by Richard Bradley*

The ABC Song - 1 - 1

# Take Me Out to the Ball Game

Words by JACK NORWORTH
Music by ALBERT VON TILZER
*Arranged by Richard Bradley*

# Baa! Baa! Black Sheep

**TRADITIONAL**
*Arranged by Richard Bradley*

© 1997 BRADLEY PUBLICATIONS
All Rights Assigned to and Controlled by BEAM ME UP MUSIC (ASCAP),
c/o WARNER BROS. PUBLICATIONS U.S. INC., 15800 N.W. 48th Avenue, Miami, FL 33014
All Rights Reserved

# This Old Man
## (Nick Nack Paddy Wack)

**TRADITIONAL**
*Arranged by Richard Bradley*

**Moderate** ♩ = 126

This old man, he played one. He played nick nack on my drum with a nick nack pad-dy-wack give the dog a bone. This old man came rol - ling home.

This old man, he played two.
This old man, he played three.
This old man, he played four.
This old man, he played five.
This old man, he played six.
This old man, he played seven.
This old man, he played eight.
This old man, he played nine.
This old man, he played ten.

He played nick nack on me shoe
He played nick nack on my knee
He played nick nack on my door
He played nick nack on my hive
He played nick nack on my sticks
He played nick nack up to heaven
He played nick nack at the gate
He played nick nack on my line
He played nick nack over again

*Chorus:*
With a nick nack paddy wack, give the dog a bone.
This old man came rolling home.

This Old Man - 1 - 1

# (Meet) The Flintstones

From the Television Series "The Flintstones"

Words and Music by
WILLIAM HANNA, JOSEPH BARBERA
and HOYT CURTIN
*Arranged by Richard Bradley*

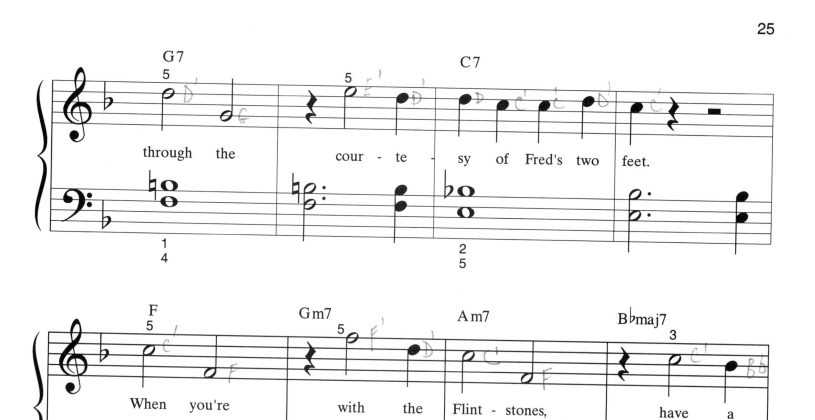

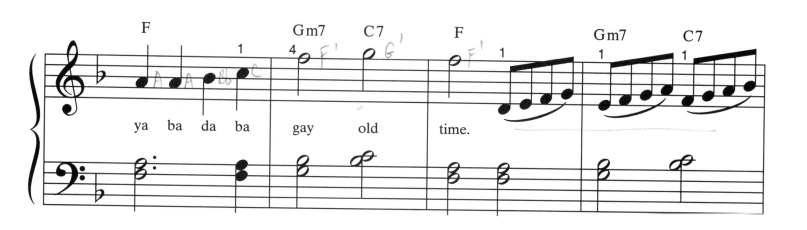

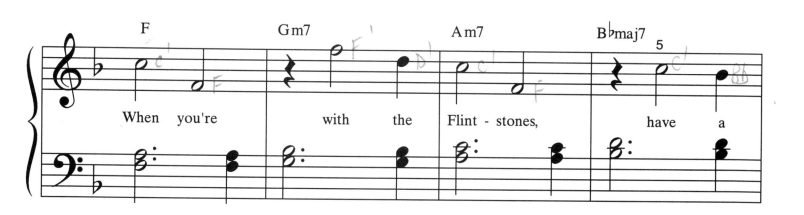

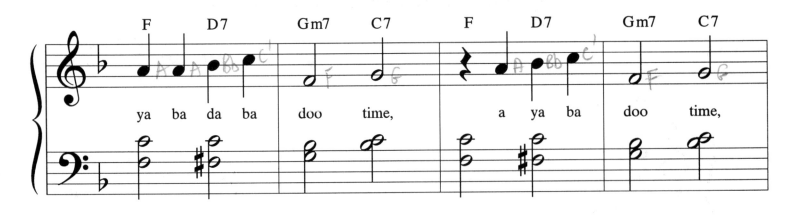

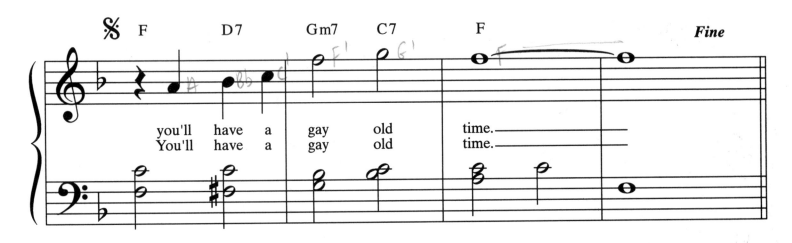

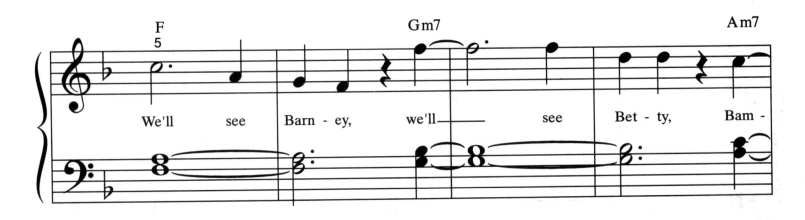

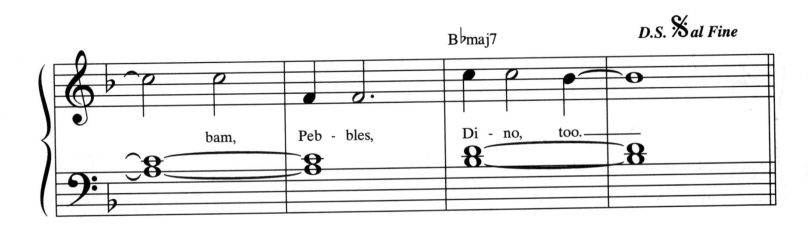

# Row, Row, Row Your Boat

TRADITIONAL
*Arranged by Richard Bradley*

**Moderate** ♩. = 96

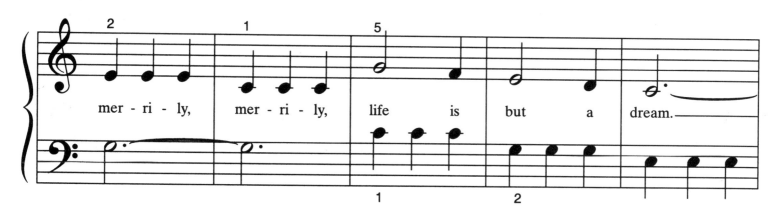

# Wakko's America

Lyrics by RANDY ROGEL
Music TRADITIONAL
*Arranged by Richard Bradley*

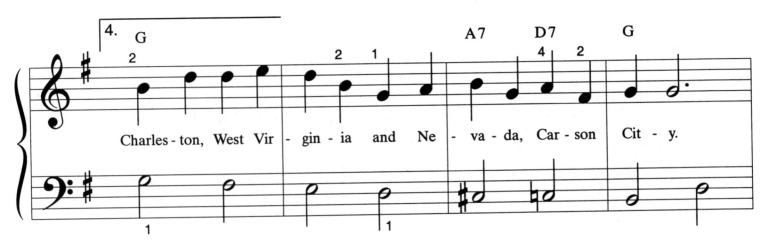

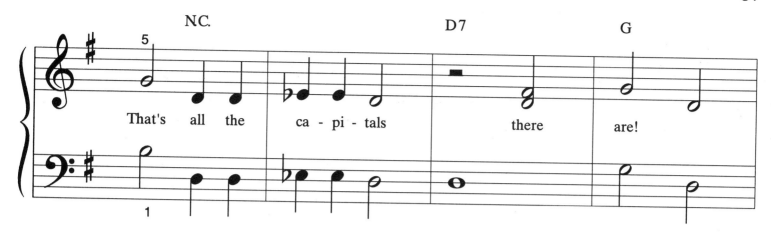

*Verse 2:*
Trenton's in New Jersey north of Jefferson, Missouri,
You got Richmond in Virginia, South Dakota has Pierre,
Harrisburg's in Pennsylvania, and Augusta's up in Maine,
And here is Providence, Rhode Island, next to Dover, Delaware.
Concord, New Hampshire, just a quick jaunt to Montpelier which is up in Vermont.
Hartford's in Connecticut, so pretty in the fall,
And Kansas has Topeka, Minneapolis has St. Paul.

*Verse 3:*
Juneau's in Alaska and there's Lincoln in Nebraska,
And it's Raleigh out in North Carolina, and then there's Madison, Wisconsin,
And Olympia in Washington, Phoenix, Arizona, and Lansing, Michigan.
Here's Honolulu, Hawaii's a joy, Jackson, Mississippi and Springfield, Illinois,
South Carolina with Columbia down the way,
And Annapolis in Maryland on Chesapeake Bay.

*Verse 4:*
Cheyenne is in Wyoming
And perhaps you make your home in Salt Lake City out in Utah where the buffalo roam.
Atlanta's down in Georgia and there's Bismark, North Dakota,
And you can live in Frankfort in your old Kentucky home.
Salem in Oregon, from there we join, Little Rock in Arkansas,
Iowa's got DesMoines, Sacramento, California,
Oklahoma and its City. . .

# She'll Be Coming 'Round the Mountain

TRADITIONAL
*Arranged by Richard Bradley*

# London Bridge

TRADITIONAL
*Arranged by Richard Bradley*

# Old MacDonald

**TRADITIONAL**
*Arranged by Richard Bradley*

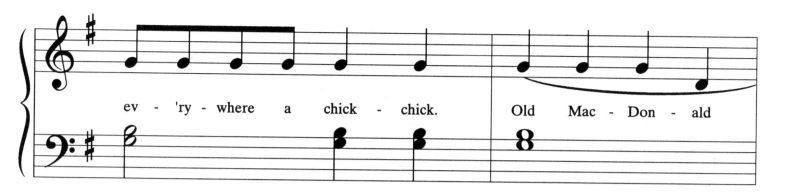

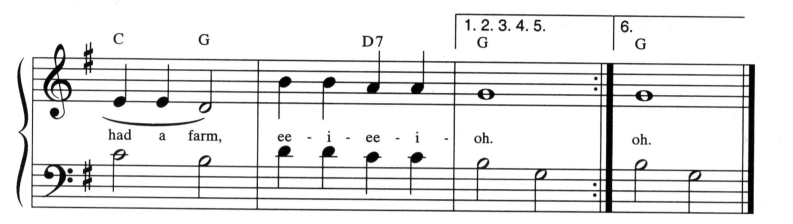

2.
Old MacDDonald had a farm,
Ee - i - ee - i - oh,
And on his farm he had some ducks,
Ee - i - ee - i - oh.
With a quack - quack here,
And a quack - quack there.
Here a quack, there a quack,
everywhere a quack - quack.
Old MacDonald had a farm,
Ee - i - ee - i - oh.

3.
Old MacDDonald had a farm,
Ee - i - ee - i - oh,
And on his farm he had some turkeys,
Ee - i - ee - i - oh.
With a gobble - gobble here,
And a gobble - gobble there.
Here a gobble, there a gobble,
everywhere a gobble - gobble.
Old MacDonald had a farm,
Ee - i - ee - i - oh.

4.
Old MacDDonald had a farm,
Ee - i - ee - i - oh,
And on his farm he had some pigs,
Ee - i - ee - i - oh.
With an oink - oink here,
And an oink - oink there.
Here an oink, there an oink,
everywhere an oink - oink.
Old MacDonald had a farm,
Ee - i - ee - i - oh.

5.
Old MacDDonald had a farm,
Ee - i - ee - i - oh,
And on his farm he had some cows,
Ee - i - ee - i - oh.
With a moo - moo here,
And a moo - moo there.
Here a moo, there a moo,
everywhere a moo - moo.
Old MacDonald had a farm,
Ee - i - ee - i - oh.

6.
Repeat 1st verse

# Merrily We Roll Along
## ("Looney Tunes" Theme)

Words and Music by
EDDIE CANTOR, MURRAY MENCHER
and CHARLES TOBIAS
*Arranged by Richard Bradley*

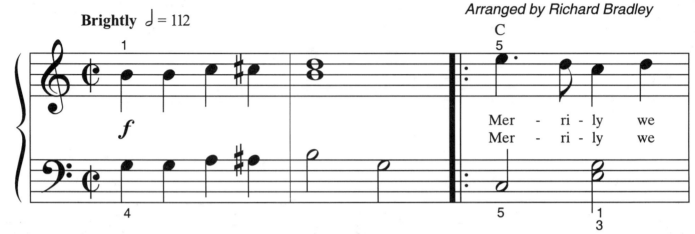

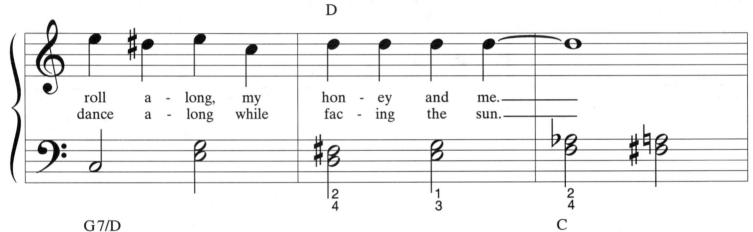

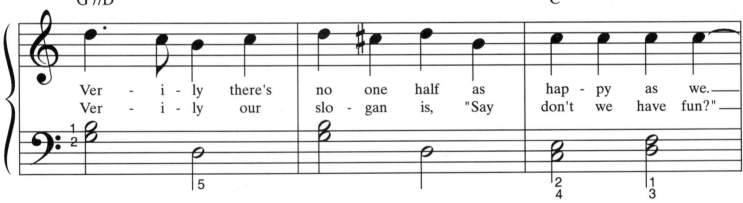

Merrily We Roll Along - 2 - 1

# chopsticks

**TRADITIONAL**
*Arranged by Richard Bradley*

© 1996 BRADLEY PUBLICATIONS
All Rights Assigned to and Controlled by BEAM ME UP MUSIC (ASCAP),
c/o WARNER BROS. PUBLICATIONS U.S. INC., 15800 N.W. 48th Avenue, Miami, FL 33014

# Alouette

**TRADITIONAL**
*Arranged by Richard Bradley*

© 1997 BRADLEY PUBLICATIONS
All Rights Assigned to and Controlled by BEAM ME UP MUSIC (ASCAP),
c/o WARNER BROS. PUBLICATIONS U.S. INC., 15800 N.W. 48th Avenue, Miami, FL 33014
All Rights Reserved

# Frère Jacques
## (Brother John)

FRENCH FOLK SONG
*Arranged by Richard Bradley*

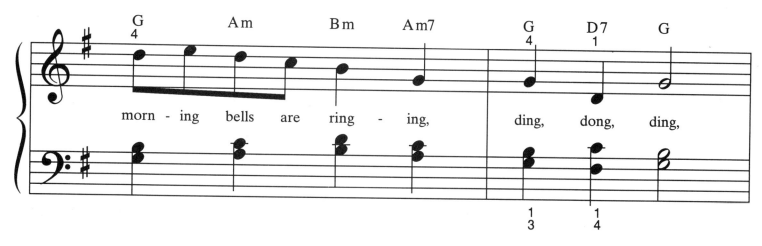

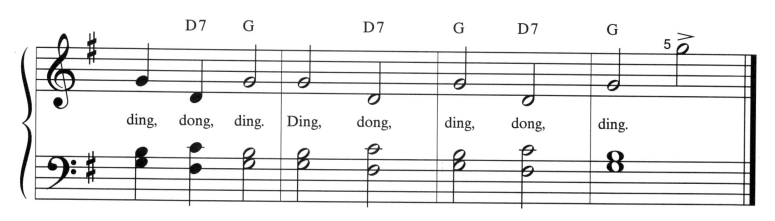

Frère Jacques - 2 - 2

# Animaniacs

Lyrics by TOM RUEGGER
Music by RICHARD STONE
*Arranged by Richard Bradley*

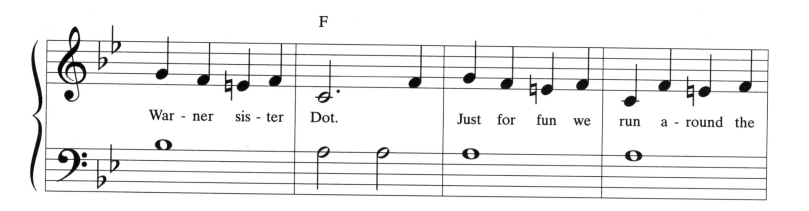

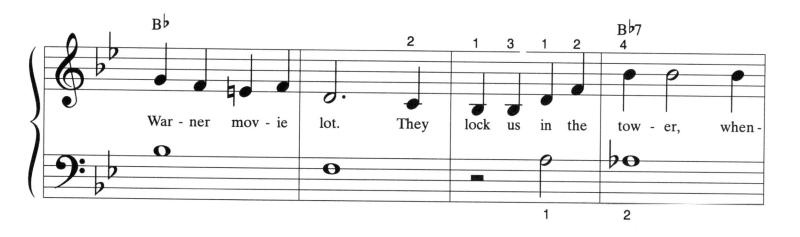

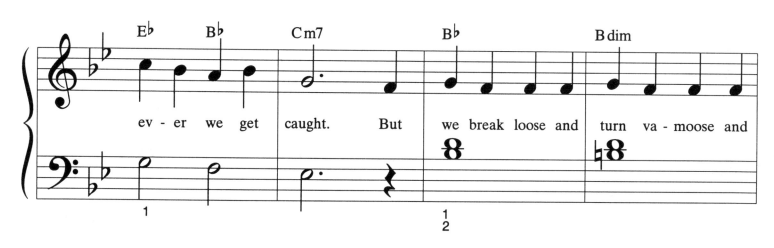

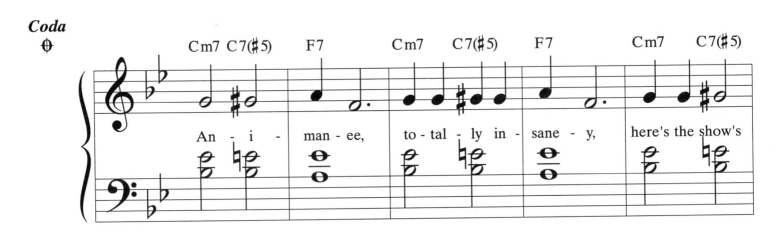

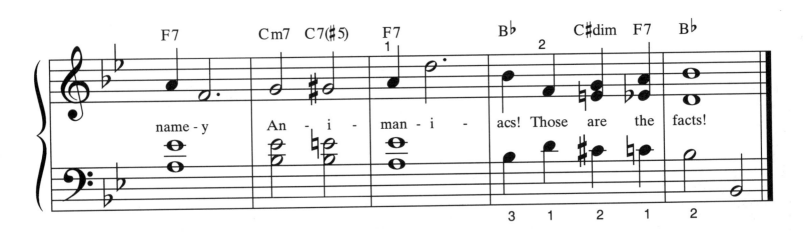

*Verse 2:*
We're Animaniacs. Dot is cute and Yakko yaks!
Wakko packs away the snacks while Bill Clinton plays the sax.
We're Animaniacs. Meet Pinky and the brain, who want to rule the Universe.
Good feathers flock together, Slappy wacks them with her purse.
Buttons chases Mindy, while Rita sings a verse.
The writers flipped, we have no script, why bother to rehearse?

*Verse 3:*
We're Animaniacs. We have pay or play contracts.
We're zany to the max; there's no baloney in our slacks.
We're Animanee, totally insaney, here's the shows namey
Animaniacs! Those are the facts!

# Peter, Peter, Pumpkin Eater

**TRADITIONAL**
*Arranged by Richard Bradley*

**Moderately** ♩ = 132  *Play notes with stems up with right hand,*
*Play notes with stems down with left hand.*

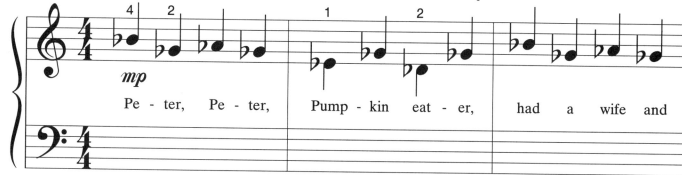

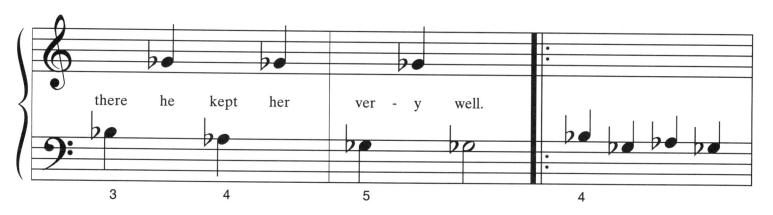

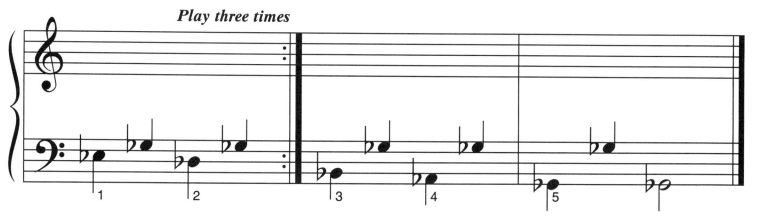

*Play three times*

Peter, Peter, Pumpkin Eater - 1 - 1

# Yogi Bear Song

From the Cartoon Television Series

Words and Music by
WILLIAM HANNA, JOSEPH BARBERA,
HOYT CURTIN and CHARLES SHOWS
*Arranged by Richard Bradley*

Yogi Bear Song - 2 - 2

# Porky "Piggeldy Wiggeldy" Pig

Words and Music by
TEDD PIERCE and WARREN FOSTER
*Arranged by Richard Bradley*

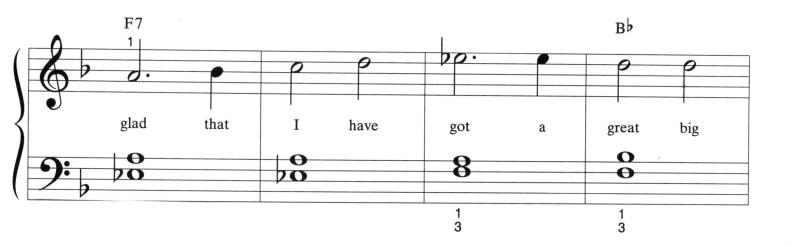

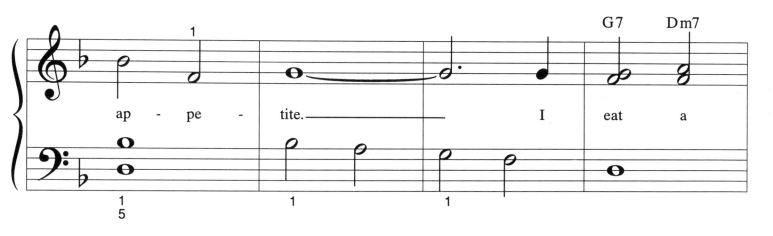

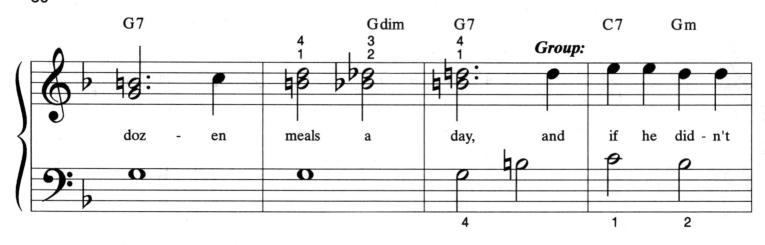

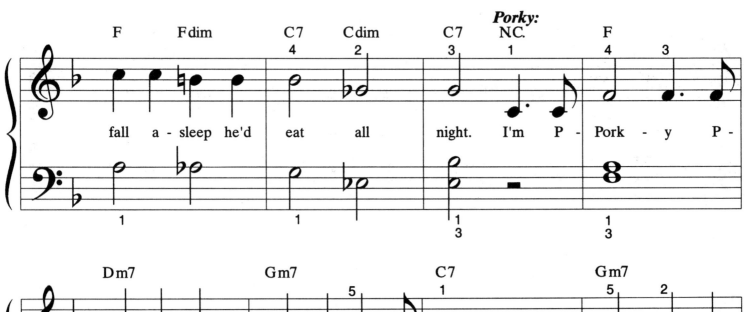

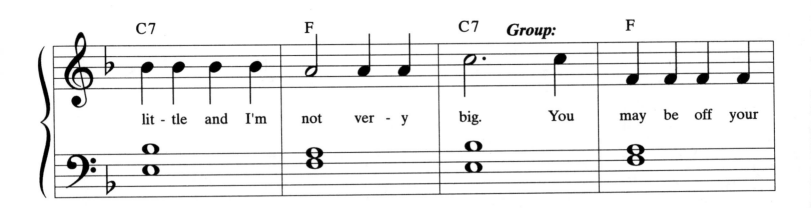

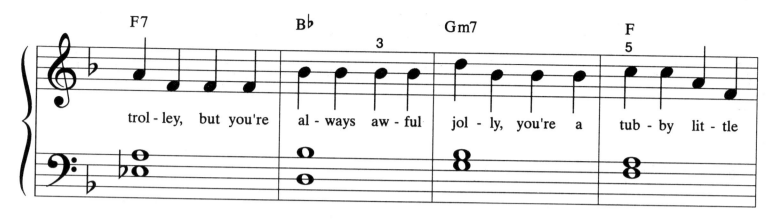

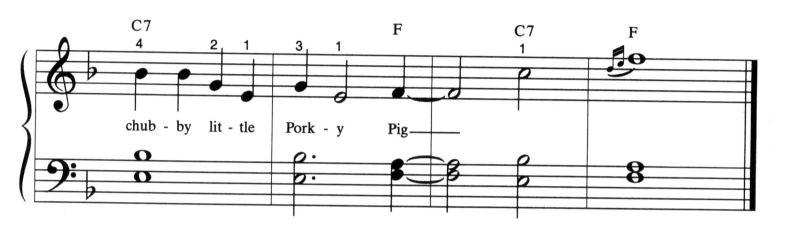

*Verse 2:*

*Porky:*
I'm P-Porky P-Piggeldy Wiggeldy P-Pig.
I like to sing a song and dance a little jig.

*Group:*
Happy as a lark and merry as a grip,
He's P-Porky P-Piggeldy Wiggeldy Pig.

# Happy Birthday to You

Words and Music by
**MILDRED J. HILL and PATTY S. HILL**
*Arranged by Richard Bradley*

# Twinkle, Twinkle, Little Star

TRADITIONAL
*Arranged by Richard Bradley*

# My Bonnie Lies Over the Ocean

TRADITIONAL
*Arranged by Richard Bradley*

My Bonnie Lies Over the Ocean - 2 - 2

# Top Cat

From the Cartoon Television Series

Words and Music by
**WILLIAM HANNA, JOSEPH BARBERA**
and **EVELYN TIMMENS**
*Arranged by Richard Bradley*

# Glow Worm

TRADITIONAL
*Arranged by Richard Bradley*

# Hush, Little Baby

TRADITIONAL
*Arranged by Richard Bradley*

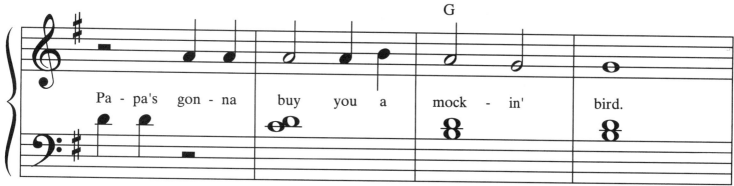

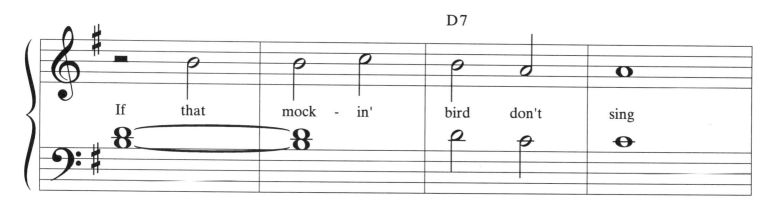

Hush, Little Baby - 1 - 1

# Talk to the Animals

From the Motion Picture *Doctor Dolittle*

Words and Music by
LESLIE BRICUSSE
*Arranged by Richard Bradley*

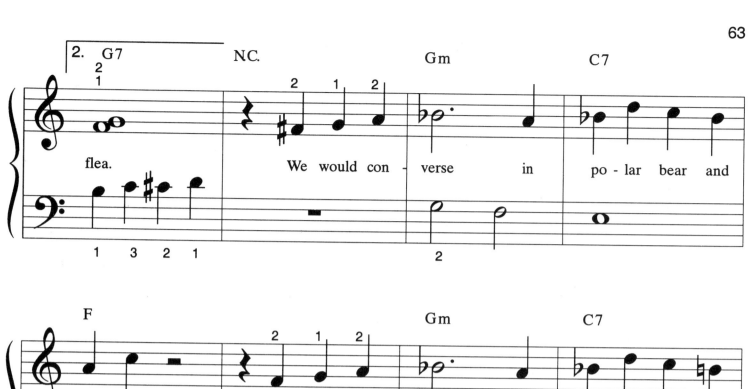

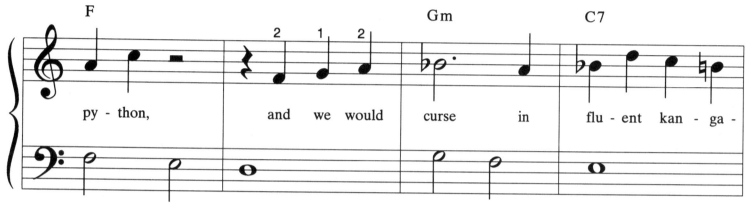

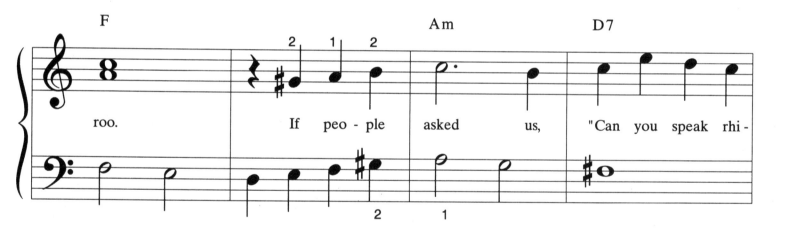

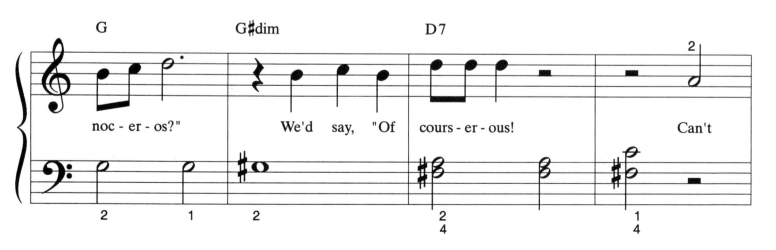

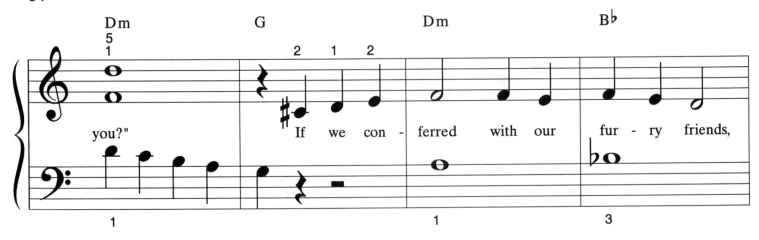

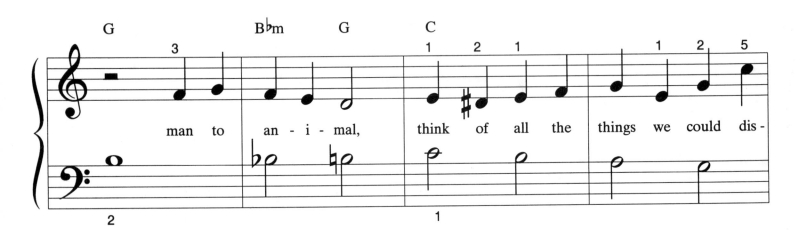

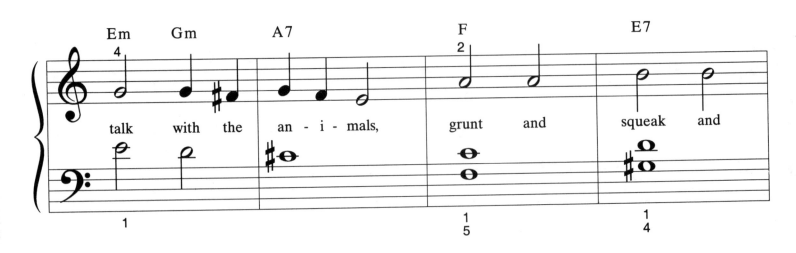

*Verse 2:*
If we could talk to the animals,
Learn their languages,
Maybe take an animal degree,
We'd study elephant and eagle,
Buffalo and beagle,
Alligator, guinea pig and flea.

# Animal Fair

**TRADITIONAL**
*Arranged by Richard Bradley*

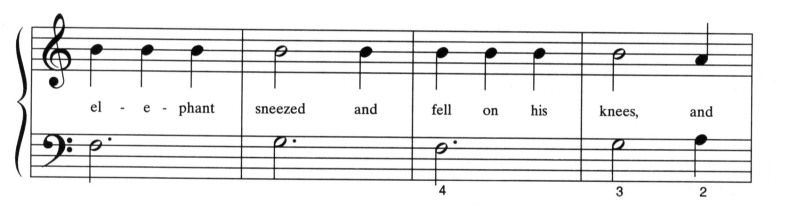

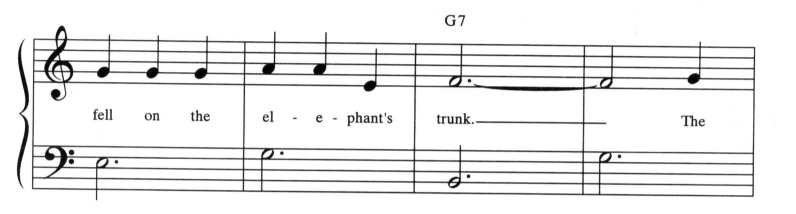

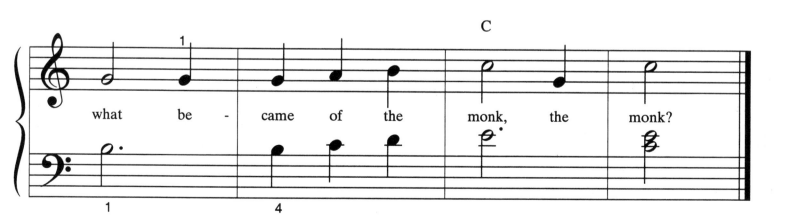

Animal Fair - 2 - 2

# Little Boy Blue

TRADITIONAL
*Arranged by Richard Bradley*

# Batman Theme

From the Television Series *Batman*
A Greenway Production in Association with 20th Century-Fox TV for ABC-TV

By
NEIL HEFTI
*Arranged by Richard Bradley*

**Moderate rock** ♩ = 96

# Tiny Toon Adventures Theme Song

Lyric by
**WAYNE KAATZ, TOM RUEGGER**
**and BRUCE BROUGHTON**

Music by
**BRUCE BROUGHTON**
*Arranged by Richard Bradley*

Tiny Toon Adventures Theme Song - 4 - 2

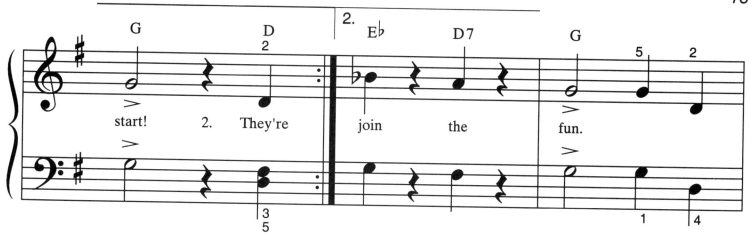

*Verse 2:*

They're furry, they're funny,
They're Babs and Buster Bunny,
Montana Max has money,
Elmyra is a pain.
Here's Hamton and Plucky,
Dizzy Devil's yucky.
Furball's unlucky
And Go-Go is insane.
At Acme Looniversity
We earn our toon degree.
The teaching staff's been getting laughs
Since Nineteen Thirty-Three.
We're tiny, we're toony,
We're all a little looney.
It's "Tiny Toon Adventures"
Come and join the fun.
And now our song is done.

# Shoo Fly!

TRADITIONAL
*Arranged by Richard Bradley*

# Pop! Goes the Weasel

**TRADITIONAL**
*Arranged by Richard Bradley*

# Jetsons Main Theme

From the Television Series *The Jetsons*

Words and Music by
**WILLIAM HANNA, JOSEPH BARBERA**
and **HOYT CURTIN**
*Arranged by Richard Bradley*

His boy El - roy.

(Spoken:) And Rosy, the robot maid.

# The Farmer in the Dell

TRADITIONAL
*Arranged by Richard Bradley*

# Sailing, Sailing

Words and Music by
GODFREY MARKS
*Arranged by Richard Bradley*

Sail - ing, sail - ing, o - ver the bound - ing main, for man - y a storm - y wind shall blow, ere Jack comes home a - gain.

# Go Go Power Rangers

Main Title from *Mighty Morphin Power Rangers*

Words and Music by
SHUKI LEVY and KUSSA MAHCHI
*Arranged by Richard Bradley*

# The Mulberry Bush

**TRADITIONAL**
*Arranged by Richard Bradley*

# Skip to My Lou

TRADITIONAL
*Arranged by Richard Bradley*

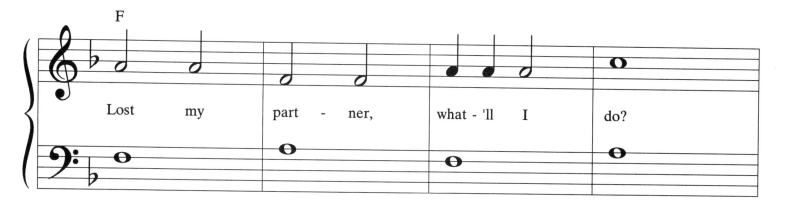

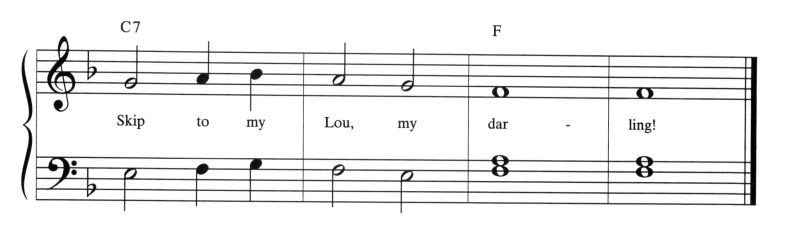

# The Bear Went Over the Mountain

TRADITIONAL
Arranged by Richard Bradley

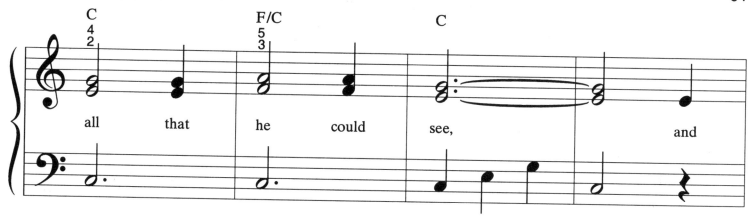

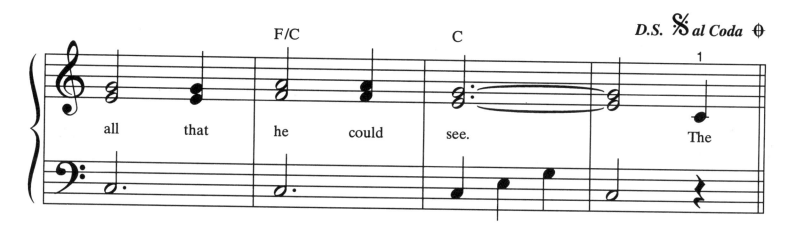

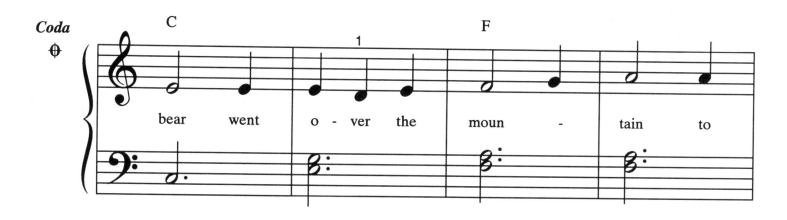

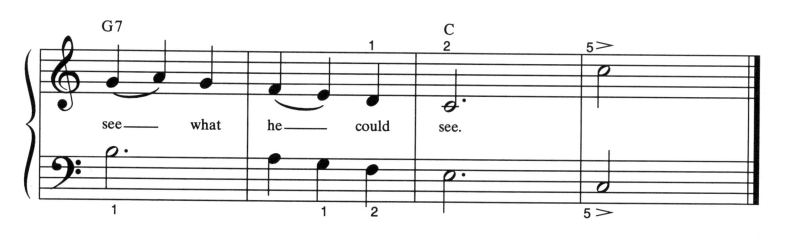

# Josie and the Pussycats
## Main Title

From the Cartoon Television Series

Words and Music by
**HOYT CURTIN, DENBY WILLIAMS**
**and JOSEPH ROLAND**
*Arranged by Richard Bradley*

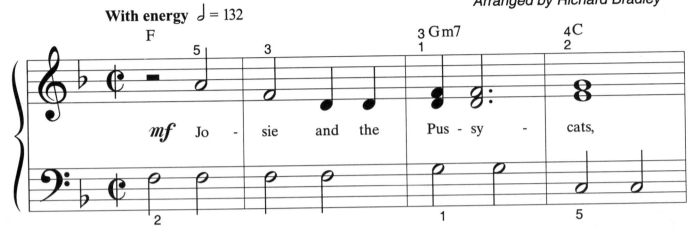

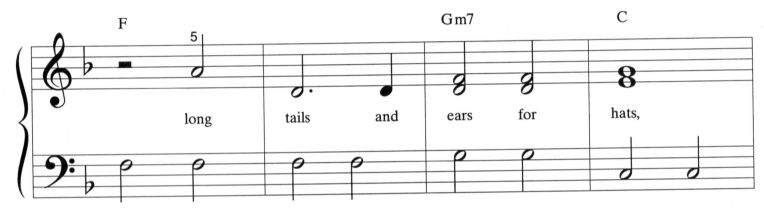

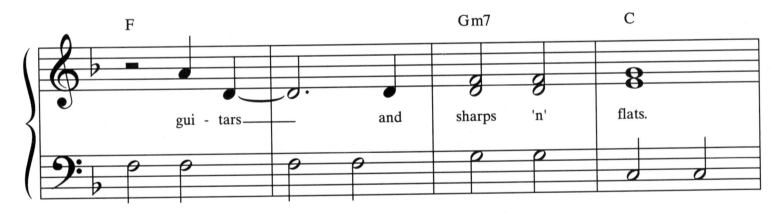

Josie and the Pussycats - 4 - 1

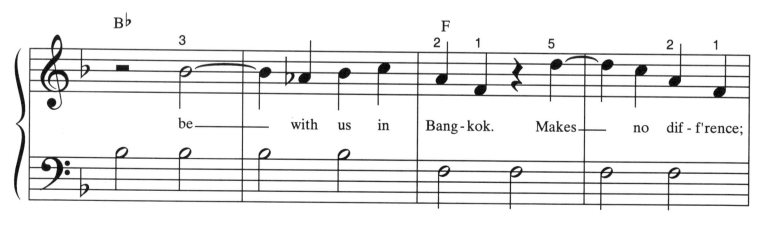

# This Is It!
## (Theme from "The Bugs Bunny Show")

Words and Music by
MACK DAVID and JERRY LIVINGSTON
Arranged by Richard Bradley

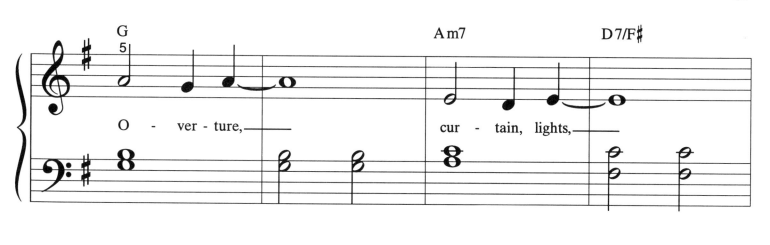

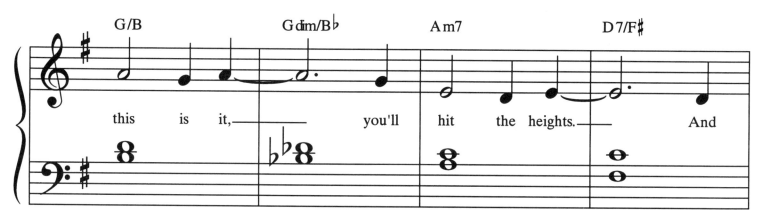

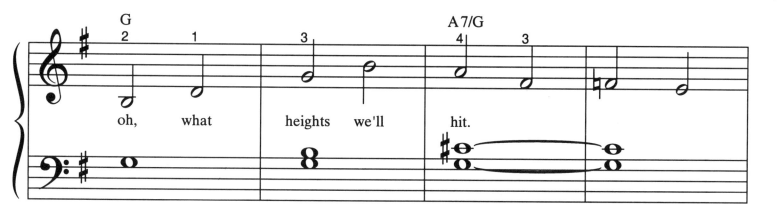

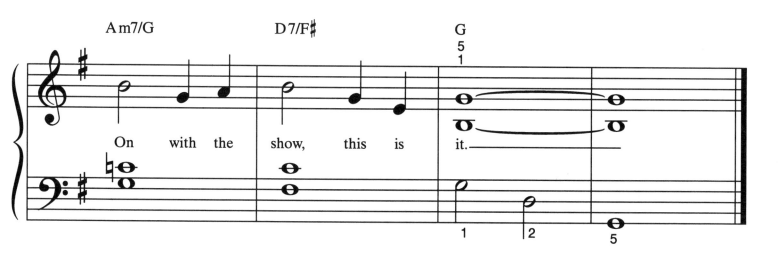

# Billy Boy

TRADITIONAL
*Arranged by Richard Bradley*

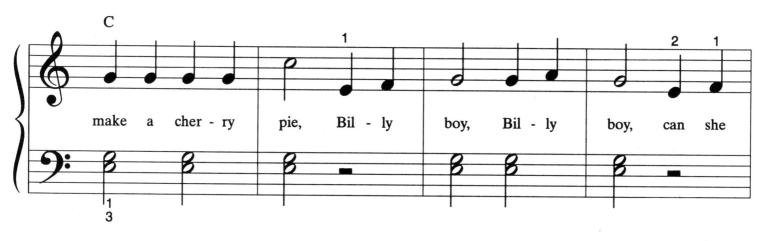

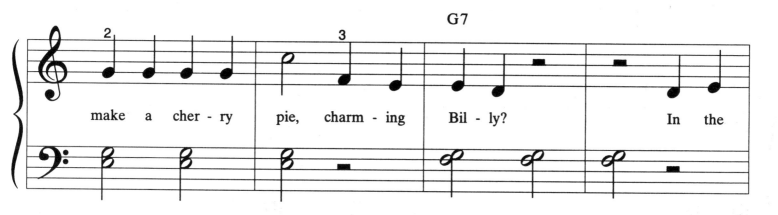

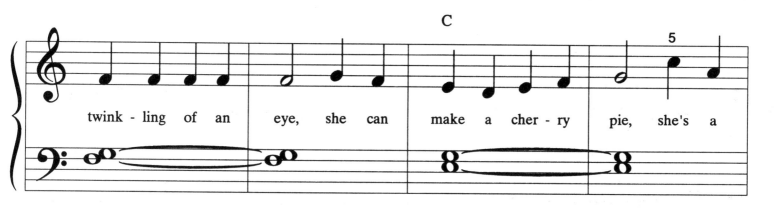

# Huckleberry Hound

From the Cartoon Television Series

Words and Music by
**WILLIAM HANNA, JOSEPH BARBERA**
**and HOYT CURTIN**
*Arranged by Richard Bradley*

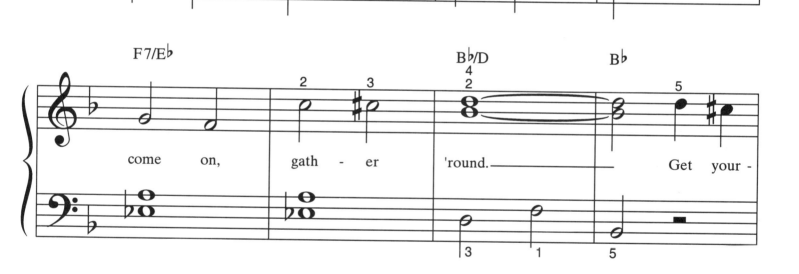

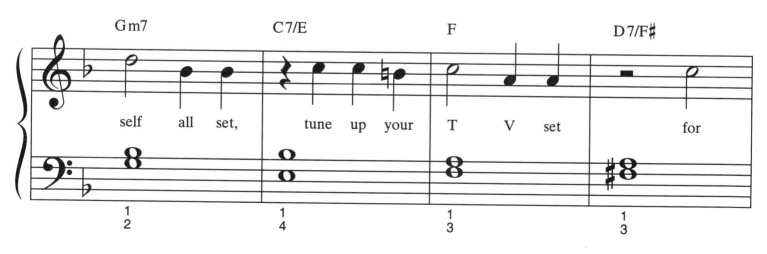

# Rock-A-Bye, Baby

**TRADITIONAL**
*Arranged by Richard Bradley*

# Three Blind Mice

**TRADITIONAL**
*Arranged by Richard Bradley*

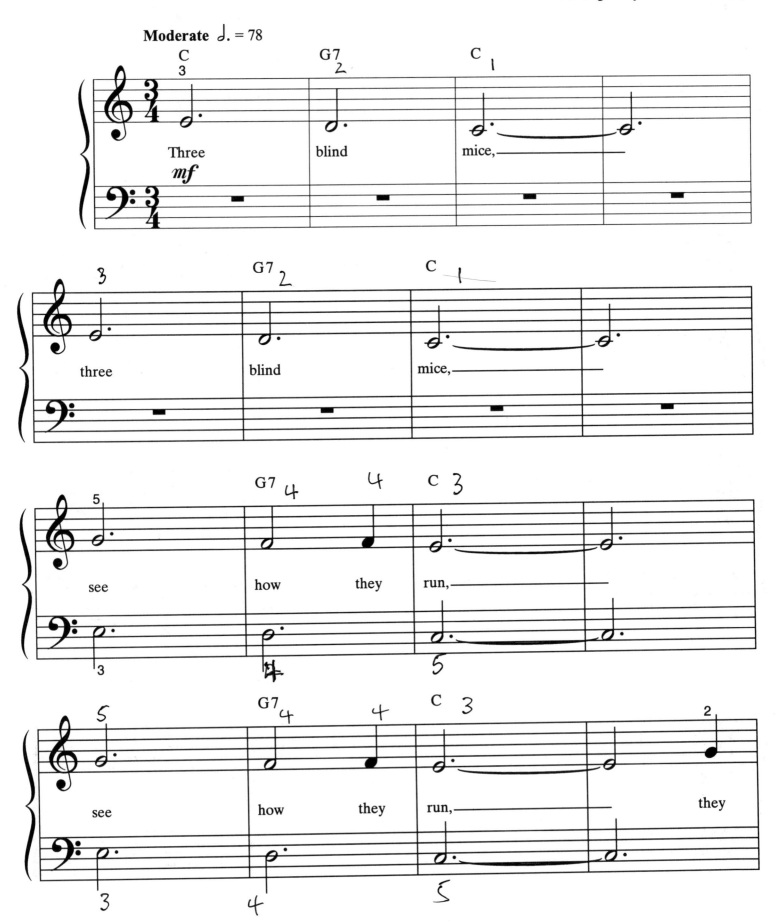

# Scooby Doo Main Title

From the Cartoon Television Series

Words and Music by
WILLIAM HANNA,
JOSEPH BARBERA and HOYT CURTIN
*Arranged by Richard Bradley*

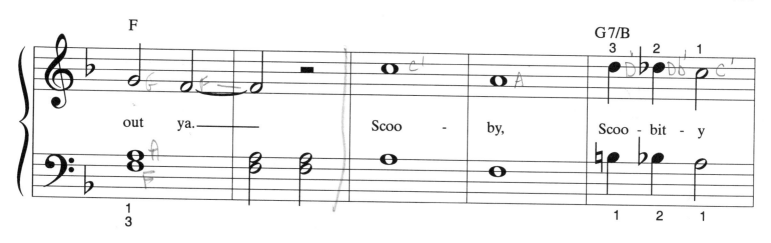

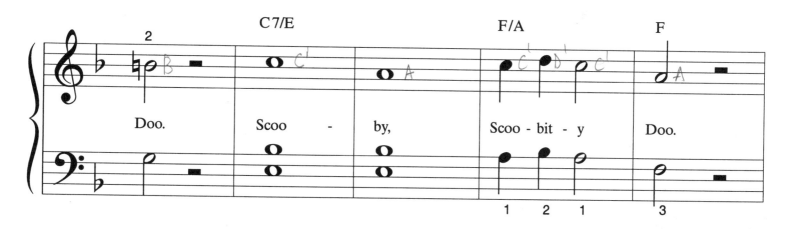

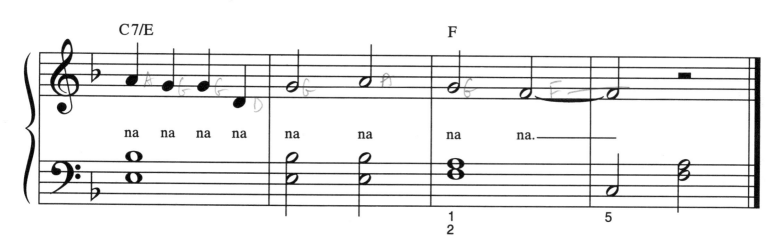

# The Teddy Bears Picnic

Words by JIMMY KENNEDY
Music by JOHN W. BRATTON
Arranged by Richard Bradley

The Teddy Bears Picnic - 2 - 1

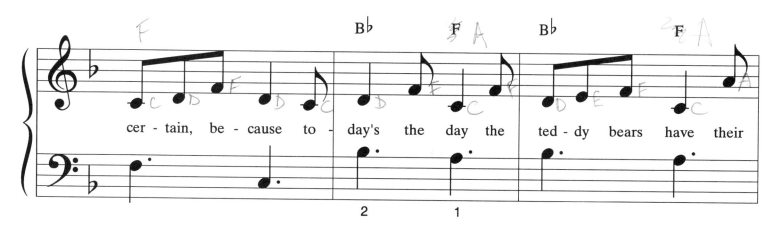

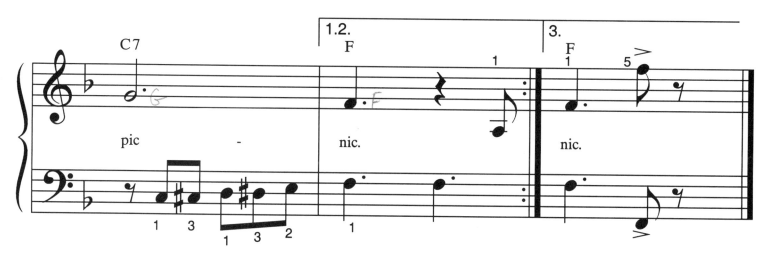

*Verse 2:*
Ev'ry teddy bear who's been good is sure of a treat today.
There's lots of marevlous things to eat, and wonderful games to play.
Beneath the trees where nobody sees, they'll hide and seek as long as they please
'Cause that's the way the teddy bears have their picnic.

*Verse 3:*
If you go down in the woods today, you'd better not go alone.
It's lovely down in the woods today but safer to stay at home.
For ev'ry bear that ever there was will gather there for certain, because
Today's the day the teddy bears have their picnic.

# Tomorrow

From the Broadway Musical and Motion Picture *Annie*

Lyric by MARTIN CHARNIN
Music by CHARLES STROUSE
*Arranged by Richard Bradley*

Tomorrow - 2 - 1

**Verse 2:**
Jus' thinking about tomorrow
Clears away the cobwebs
And the sorrow
Till there's none.

**Verse 3:**
Oh! the sun'll come out tomorrow,
So you got to hang on
Till tomorrow
Come what may!

# Where, Oh Where, Has My Little Dog Gone?

**TRADITIONAL**
*Arranged by Richard Bradley*